© 2022 VERNON WHITAKER
WE ARE SPIRITUAL BEINGS HAVING HUMAN EXPERIENCES

All rights reserved. No part of this publication may be reproduced, stored in a retrieval system, or transmitted in any form or by any means, electronic, mechanical, photocopying, recording or otherwise without the prior permission of the publisher or in accordance with the provisions of the Copyright, Designs, and Patents Act 1988 or under the terms of any license permitting limited copying issued by the Copyright Licensing Agency.

The views expressed in this work are solely those of the author and do not necessarily reflect the views of the publisher, the publisher hereby disclaims any responsibility for them.

ISBN-13: 978-1-949105-46-9 (paperback)
ISBN-13: 978-1-949105-47-6 (eBook)

\\\\\\\\\

Published by:
Divine Works Publishing
Royal Palm Beach, Florida USA
561-990-BOOK (2665)

www.DivineWorksPublishing.com

CONTENTS

Chapter 1 The Beginning | *1*

Chapter 2 The Image of God | 7

Chapter 3 The Realm of Emotions | 23

Chapter 4 Free Will to Make Choices | 35

Chapter 5 The New Garden of Eden | 41

Chapter 6 The Invisible God Inside of You | 45

INTRODUCTION
WE ARE SPIRITUAL BEINGS HAVING A HUMAN EXPERIENCE

I want to introduce you to who you really are. You are a spirit being who God Himself fashioned in His own image and likeness. You, *as a spiritual being,* can live fruitfully in the God created physical world in turn glorifying the handiwork of God. God created a physical world that needed a physical man to extol the spiritual world of God. God created a physical man's body out of this physical world, and this physical body houses his spirit to enjoy, explore, and advance the physical world. God blew into the nostrils of a lifeless physical man to house the spirit man and he become alive. God created this living soul to have human experiences. This book is written to unpack how you are a spiritual being living in a physical body that has the form of a living soul. From your living soul, God can enjoy your worship and relationship with Him. Each experience you experience as a spiritual being, results in you reacting from your human emotions. So, Jesus came into the physical world in a human body and experienced your human emotions. You, as a spiritual being, experienced what sin is. So Jesus experienced the human experience of sin without succumbing to sin itself. Jesus did not physically commit any sin while He was in the physical world. *1 Peter 2:22 "He committed no sin, and no deceit was found in His mouth."*

CHAPTER ONE

THE BEGINNING

If you think that once you die that you are dead, then you don't understand death. The spirit on the inside of your physical dust body cannot die. During death of the physical body there is a release of the spirit and soul from the physical body.

> *"Behold, I shew you a mystery;*
> *We shall not all sleep, but we shall all be changed,"*
> —*1 Corinthians 15:51*

So death is nothing more than you are asleep before your spiritual being and soul depart from your physical body. Some of you will not be asleep at all for the changing of your spirit being and soul enters into another physical body. Your physical body is not truly yours; it belongs to planet earth. You can call it your own while you reside in it, but it does not belong to you.

I want to use the Bible as the only authority on understanding your body, soul, and spirit and why you are living right now. You have no clue about your body, your soul, and your spirit being as you are having human experiences in this physical world. Your spirit being was before your physical body.

> *"Before I formed thee in the belly I knew thee;*
> *and before thou camest forth out of the womb I sanctified thee,*
> *and I ordained thee a prophet unto the nations."*
> *—Jeremiah 1:5*

Your spirit being was with God long before your physical body was created. Your spirit being was with God before the foundation of the earth. Your physical body was created by God for your spirit being. Your physical body has one function and that is to house your soul and your spirit being.

> *"And the Lord God formed man of the dust of the ground, and breathed into his nostrils the breath of life; and man became a living soul." —Genesis 2:7*

Through God's divine power of creation, He releases your spirit being with your soul into your temple of dust. Your physical body is connected to this planet as it is formed out of the same molecular structure of the planet earth. What did God blow into the nostrils of the lifeless piece of clay to make it a living soul? What causes your living soul to have feelings, emotions, and intelligence? There is something more to you that even you don't know, what God has placed on the inside of you.

Some might debate over which God created first, your body or your spirit being?

This raises the question, "what is a spirit being?" According to the dictionary, a spiritual being is defined as *"an incorporeal being believed to have powers to affect the course of human events."* To affect human events God created spirit beings in the image and likeness of Himself.

Watch this: Genesis 1:26 "And God said, Let us make man in Our image, after Our Likeness: and let them have dominion over the fish of the sea, and over the fowl of the air, and over the cattle, and over the earth, and over every creeping thing that creepeth upon the earth."

You existed on the inside of God first before you were housed in your body. The reason God makes you first a spiritual being is because God is a Spirit being, The purpose of making you in the image of God is to introduce the atmosphere of heaven into His physical world. The angels could not fulfill this operation in the physical world. If God has total dominion over the entirety of creation and everything that He created, that includes you as a spirit being, then you are created a spirit being whom God gave dominion over this earth since you are His image and likeness in order to rule this world. There is no way that you were made a spirit being after the image and likeness of God himself that you don't have dominion and authority to operate in the world God created. That would make you a powerless spirit being in the image and likeness of God. As a spirit being you are having human experiences in the physical world. God wants you to experience this wonderful world that He created for you, but you need a body to move about in this wonderful world of God. Your human flesh was created to experience the reality of this great creation.

The reality of the world is that you feel the wind blowing on your flesh. You see with your eyes colors of every object that you see. The green in trees, the blue in water, the white in clouds, and the color of skin of different people. The reality is real when you hear the sound of your children crying, the sound of the wind in the trees, the sound of your footsteps as you walk across the floor. This is the reality of God's physical world that you are in.

God did all this according to His plan and purpose to make you a spirit being. That you would have a body, soul, and a spirit. Since God created the physical world, and placed you as a spirit being within a physical body to move and operate in this physical world legally. When God speaks a word it becomes a law. When God spoke "let us make man in our image and likeness" you became a law that was manifest as a spiritual being. The other part of that law was that you, a spirit being, will have dominion over the physical world. That part of the law of dominion was manifest in the physical world, by the work of the Holy Ghost, the Spirit of God. Therefore, God took His spoken law of dominion and you a spirit being, dressed you in a physical body, that God fashioned by His own hands. So the law of dominion and you, a spirit being, can do God work in this physical world.

Genesis 2:7 said, *"And the Lord formed man of the dust of the ground, and breathed into his nostrils the breath of life; and man became a living soul."* God created your body into something unique that would not naturally evolve. God formed a physical body out of dust of the earth and that dust body was to house you, a spirit being. That was the only way that you can operate in this world legally through a physical body. So God, in His great power, breathed into that dust body your spirit being and living soul. So, the combination of the spirit man and dust body became a living soul that is called human.

CHAPTER TWO

THE IMAGE OF GOD

For you then, *as a spirit being*, is now authorized to experience human experiences. Don't miss this part, when God, in His breath, blew your spirit into your temple, God also blew His Spiritual DNA directly into the nostrils of a dust man. Pay attention! God never says a word over that dust man to make him come alive. God never spoke directly to that dust man and said, "come alive." It was God's DNA mixed with your spirit being which caused the lifeless body to merge with your spirit being and soul and caused the things inside of the man to come alive. The heart began beating, the lungs began to breathe, the brain began to think thoughts, blood began to flow like a river, cells began to grow, strength came in to the man's body, and the eyes of man opened to see all that God created. Now, you are a live human being housing a spirit being. With God's DNA your soul possesses the ability to have senses, emotions, and intelligence.

If you are the spitting image of God then you have God senses, emotions, and intelligence to operate into this world. You are the only creature that is made after the image and likeness of God and the purpose of this is to bring God's glory and heavenly culture into this physical world.

God combines the spirit being, soul, and the dust body to enter into this physical world, so that the spirit being may undergo a human experience which the angels of heaven cannot. The human experience that God was looking from the spirit being in the dust body is to have a human soul experience with Him in fellowship. In this human experience that you have as a spirit being received in the physical world is the ability to *experience* your life and life lessons. Your soul's human experience rose well above that of the angels in heaven. In that you, *a spirit being*, is able to have human emotions, divine knowledge, and the ability to reproduce after your own kind.

What makes it legal for God to operate in this physical world is a physical body. Because God's law gives the spiritual being daimonion over this world, and that took God out of operating in this physical world. And God is a Spirit, it is illegal for God to operate on this earth without a physical body. God cannot go against the law of daimonion and the principle of the physical world. God cannot go against His word that is law. God is limited by His word because His word is above Him. In Genesis 1:26 is where the law was made, *"And let them have dominion"* and that law was given to you a spirit before you entered into your dust body. Physical man is the authority to operate in this physical world. Your purpose is to bring the culture of heaven, into the earth. "That is powerful!"

If you look at Matthew 6:9-10, When Jesus taught the manner of prayer we ought to pray is, "Our Father which art in heaven, Hallowed be thy name. Thy kingdom come, Thy will be done in earth, as it is in heaven." This is to say that the will of God the Father be done in earth as it is done in heaven. That His will be done in this physical world. Not the will of men, nor the will of satan, nor the will of wicked men, but God's own will. As a spiritual being, living in your dust temple, operating in this physical world, you must let the will of heaven loose in this world to bring order and the culture of the almighty God into this confused world. Heaven is in order and peace. So, you must bring order and peace back to this world, like it was before the days of Adam, before sin was brought into the garden. The will of the Father will stamp out sin once and for all.

God removed Himself from the equation when He spoke "let them have dominion." God said, I will not intervene with man because it is your work to bring My glory into this world. You know without man God cannot bring His glory to the earth. Without God man is not the glory of God created to bring the heavenly culture in this physical world.

Any spirit operating in this physical world without a body is operating illegally. This is what Satan knows that it is illegal to operate against the principle of the physical world without a body. Satan gave his demons the authorization to use any human body to operate legally in this world. Satan's trick is to get your soul man to become dark in disobedience to God. Your natural man subdues your soul man by putting out your light of righteousness. When you give in to darkness you are giving Satan authority to use your body for his evil work against you. When you become light, that is when your soul man subdues your natural man, and that gives God the authority to use your human body to do spiritual works through you, (who is a spirit being). God made it where you, as a spirit being, in this physical world, are having a human experience in order to obtain the knowledge of the glory of God.

God spoke the law of dominion into existence in Genesis 1:28, "And God blessed them, and God said unto them, Be fruitful, and multiply, and replenish the earth, and subdue it: and have dominion over the fish of the sea, and over the fowl of the air, and over every living thing that moveth upon the earth."

Genesis 2:19, "And out of the ground the Lord God formed every beast of the field and every fowl of the air, and brought them unto Adam to see what he would call them: and whatsoever Adam called every living creature, that was the name thereof.

This is the glory of God, when God formed every living creature, He gave you, a spiritual being, the first human experience in authority by delegating the responsibility of naming all the animals which fill the earth. God gave you, a spiritual being, the ability to name every living creature and God did not step in to change any name of these living creatures. This is the first human experience in exercising authority in the physical world. Speaking with your God, by using your authority to name the animals is the glory of God. Man was working to establish God's heavenly kingdom on earth. God's divine purpose was not to interfere with Adam naming the animals because it was illegal for God to step in after the law of dominion was given unto Adam over this earth. And God's word is law. In Psalm 138:2 "I will worship toward Thy holy temple, and praise Thy name for Thy loving kindness and: for Thy hast magnified Thy word above all Thy name." God could not go against His word because His word is above Him.

The next spirit being human experience you undertake in your dust body is a God sanctified marriage. God gave the man and the woman the ability to have sex and reproduce after the *spirit being* kind, to fill the earth with God's Glory.

Sexual intimacy is to the Glory of God to help bring the heavenly culture into this physical world. Spirit beings, God made them, male and female and where command by the law of God to reproduce by having sex with one another. Sex in marriage is to glorify God's design and fulfill the procreation law. In marriage it is to be intimate with one another. To have companionship with one another in this physical world. This companionship will bring about a relationship within oneness with God. Physical pleasure is to be experienced by spiritual beings in a clay body experience.

"For in the resurrection they neither marry, nor are given in marriage, but are as the angels of God in heaven." |
—*Matthew 22:30*

Angels are not made out of the earth as natural beings. God created them as beings that cannot procreate. If they could, don't you think God would have allowed angels to reproduce with each other. Instead of creating untold numbers of them? If Satan could procreate, then Satan would not need you to do his evil work. Satan then could reproduce evil after himself. Satan would not need God's kingdom, he would make his own kingdom.

The next spirit being human experience you have in your dust body is a love experience.

> "Let thy fountains be blessed: and rejoice with the wife of thy youth. Let her be as the loving hind and pleasant rose; let her breasts satisfy thee at all times; and be thou ravished always with her love." —Proverbs 5:18-19

Adam, the spirit man, had full authority over the world and everything in it. But, Adam needed the love and championship of another human being of the other sex.

God never intended for humankind to deviate from the intended nature of man and woman. You, a spiritual being, was never authorized to covet someone else's husband or wife nor to have sex with animals. That is why God said in Genesis 2:18, "And the Lord, God said, it is not good that the man should be alone : I will make him an help meet for him." God knew that the spiritual being in a dust body would long for a mate to be with. God did not want man to have sex with the animals nor men with men nor women with women, that was not God design for man.

> "For this cause God gave them up unto vile affections: for even their women did change the natural use into that which is against nature: And likewise also the men, leaving the natural use of the woman, burned in their lust one toward another; men with men working that which is unseemly, and receiving in themselves that recompence of their error which was meet."
> —Romans 1:26-27,

These acts of men with men and women with women defile the law that God set for the spiritual being to experience the human experience. The purpose of sex was to fulfill God's original design to reproduce and replenish the earth with humankind in order for man to fellowship with God.

Man and woman are designed to have sex with one wife or husband for the rest of your life experience in this physical world. When you have sex outside of marriage, they are your wife or husband in the spirit. John 4:15-18 15 The woman saith unto him, Sir, give me this water, that I thirst not, neither come hither to draw. 16 Jesus saith unto her, Go, call thy husband, and come hither. 17 The woman answered and said, I have no husband. Jesus said unto her, Thou hast well said, I have no husband: 18 For thou hast had five husbands; and he whom thou now hast is not thy husband: in that saidst thou truly. Jesus told her that all those men she slept with are married to her spiritually. But by the law of marriage, you do not have a husband that you can call your own.

God's purpose for man, was to reproduce after his own kind like God made after His kind. Therefore, God formed the marriage institution so that spiritual beings can go through the human experience in oneness. God put man to sleep, and took his wife from his rib.

"and the Lord God cause a deep sleep to fall upon Adam, and he slept: and He took one of his ribs, and close up the flesh instead therefore; And the rib, which the Lord God had taken from man, made He a woman, and brought her unto the man. And Adam said, This is now bone of my bones, and flesh of my flesh:

she shall be called woman, because she was taken out of man."
—Genesis 2:20-23

Your wife's spiritual man is part of you. You must love your wife.

"Husbands, love your wives, even as Christ also loved the church, and gave himself for it." —Ephesians 5:25

Your spiritual man, in your experience of human love, gives all of your love to your one and only wife. As Jesus gave his all for the one and only church. God went as far as taking man's wife from the man's body. So Adam would have an inborn passion towards his wife because she is a part of him.

Adam, in his passion and love for his wife, called her woman, as in being a part of him to glorify God. As God and Jesus are in *oneness*, so should a husband and his wife be. Adam, *the spirit being*, has human experiences filled with passion and love for his wife. You can see the love that Adam has for his wife in verse 24 of Genesis 2 when Adam said, *"Therefore shall a man leave his father and his mother, and shall cleave unto his wife: and they shall be one flesh."* Adam had the power and the authority to name his wife as he named the animals.

"And Adam called his wife's name Eve: because she was the mother of all living." —Genesis 3:20

That why it is a sin against God for two men or two women to have sex together. This sin is against God's law of reproduction for the spiritual being to have that experience.

In this human experience of sex between man and woman, God created the institution of marriage. But Adam called his rib woman, his wife which will always be a part of him. That God Himself ordains the man and the woman to enjoy one another in this pleasure. And the fruit of their pleasure is to reproduce after their own kind to glorify God within God's guidelines for marriage. God's institution of marriage was never intended to be between man and man or woman and woman.

God instituted marriage, but Adam set up the rule for marriage to come in the future physical world so that every spiritual being should follow. That every man shall leave his father and mother and cling to his wife with a passionate love toward his wife. This is the human experience you are to experience as a spirit being in this physical world.

"And Jesus answering said unto them, The children of this world marry and are given in marriage: But they which shall be accounted worthy to obtain that world, and the resurrection from the dead, neither marry, nor are given in marriage: neither can they die any more: for they are equal unto the angels; and are the children of God, being the children of the resurrection."
—Luke 20:34-36

This explains why you marry in this physical world, in the present now, because you are mortal men. You marry to leave an inheritance for your children as you reproduce them. But in the resurrection, there will be no need to marry, to procreate any children to keep mankind going. You will receive your adopted body in the resurrection by grace, so you are the children of God into eternal life.

This explains why angels do not marry or reproduce like you the spirit being in your dust body. When God created the angels, God created enough Angels so that there would always be enough angels to minister to you the spirit being in your dust body on this earth. Psalm 103:20 *"Bless the Lord, ye His angels, that excel in strength, that do His commandments, hearkening unto the voice of His word."* These angels are to do whatever God wanted the angels to do in Heaven.

Since God did not need to ever increase in the number of angels, therefore, there was no need for God to give the Angels the ability to reproduce offspring.

What is so special about you is the spirit being in your dust body that God Himself loves so much, and gives you the spirit being in your dust body the authorization over God creation. That the other spirits in heaven were not able to have. No other spiritual beings or angels are named in the Bible of having the authorization over God creation. God gave you the spirit beings to judge angels according to His word.

> *"Do ye not know that the saints shall judge the world? And if the world shall be judged by you, are ye unworthy to judge the smallest matters? Know ye not that we shall judge angels? How many more things that pertain to this life?"*
> —1 Corinthians 6:2-3

Those angels to be judged are the evil angels and the devil. Not that you the spirit beings will judge their future final judgment and condemnation on the last day. But you the spiritual being approve of the sentence pronounced upon them and their destruction of the judgment of them. And of their ejection out of the world.

Because you, the spirit being God, realize that one of your next spiritual being human experiences would be loneliness. And in your loneliness, there would be pain associated with it. God created all the other animals with a mate and this spirit man in this dust body had no mate. Although God would have fellowship with you spirit man, God realizes that you the spirit man would go through the process of loneliness and pain. This process of loneliness would begin because you spiritual man disobeyed God's word. Genesis 3 tells us that the woman and man eat fruit off the tree good and evil and their eyes are open to the pleasure of the world. And they found themselves naked and they hid themselves for God.

Genesis 3:24 tells us *"So He drove out the man; and He placed at the east of the garden of Eden Cherubims, and a flaming sword which turned every way, to keep the way of the tree of life."* This is the beginning of the process of loneliness and the pain of not having fellowship with God. Because you, *the spirit man,* was not in harmony with his natural man and soul in your body. That causes you to be out of balance with God. That is when the portal that Satan needs to be opened to bring in disobey onto humankind.

The door of loneliness and pain is open now for you, the spirit being to experience pain in your life, until you are called back home to the spiritual world. It all starts at Genesis 3:17-19, *"And unto Adam He said, Because thou hast hearkened unto the voice of thy wife, and hast eaten of the tree, of which I commanded thee, saying, Thou shalt not eat of it: cursed is the ground for thy sake; in sorrow shalt thou eat of it all the days of thy life: Thorns also and thistles shall it bring forth to thee; and thou shall eat the herb of the field; In the sweat of thy face shalt thou eat bread, till thou return unto the ground; for out of it wast thou taken: for dust thou art, and unto dust shalt thou return."* Adam did the opposite of the word of God. Which Adam ought to have been obedient to God's word. All things which you, *the spirit being,* once had possession and dominion over shifted when sin entered in and now many trials and trouble ensue in cultivating the earth. You, *the spirit being*, were not permitted to eat of the fruits of the garden of Eden, but to eat only of the common field of herbs. Your body is composed of dust; it shall be reduced back to the original form of dust.

In your human experience of loneliness and pain, God will not let you die spiritually. *This is a promise that if you submit everything to God that your soul man will not be separate from Him.* That when you are raised with a new body, not like your old dust body but a glorified body.

"It is sown a natural body;
it is raised a spiritual body." —1 Corinthians 15:44

There is a natural body, and there is a spiritual body. Your natural body then will be subject to your spirit and soul. Your spiritual body then will worship God in spiritual service, the recourse is there is no more spiritual warfare. Your spiritual body will be fitted and assisted by the Holy Ghost so that you will delight with spiritual things. Your spiritual body will live without natural help and will never die. The Holy Ghost does this intervention according to God's purpose and plan. Jesus experienced loneliness and pain in the Garden of Gethsemane.

"My soul is exceeding sorrowful, even unto death. If it be possible, let this cup pass from me: nevertheless not as I will, but as thou will." —Matthew 26:36-39

Jesus shows us even when your soul man experiences human loneliness and pain how to submit to God's will. In submitting to God that will compensate for your loneliness. The only recourse is to turn to God and plead for mercy, giving God the permission to intervene on your behalf. And that is your only hope is in God. Jesus once again experienced human loneliness and pain in Matthew 27:46 Jesus asked the question of His Father in the ninth hour of the human experience of loneliness and pain *"Eli, Eli, lama sabachthani?* That is to say, My God, My God, why hast Thou forsaken Me? Jesus was looking for God to intervene with His plea for mercy. Jesus shows us in the midst of darkness your soul must surrender to the will of God even unto death. In this you will overcome your flesh man to have victory over your human experience of loneliness and pain.

Here again Jesus shows you in your soul the experience of loneliness and pain that you still need to trust in God the Father. Luke 23:46 reads, *"And when Jesus had cried with a loud voice, He said, Father, into Thy hands I commend My spirit and having said thus, He gave up the ghost."* Jesus in the natural entrusted God, His Father, with His spirit. When His spirit leaves His dust body, that His spirit would be resurrected to make that journey back home to His Father with God's intervention. Jesus was sold out in nature by submitting everything that He had to God the Father. He commits His spirit, soul, and body to God.

> "But if Christ is in you, then even though your body is subject to death because of sin, Spirit gives life because of righteousness. And if the Spirit of him who raised Jesus from the dead is living in you, he who raised Christ from the dead will also give life to your mortal bodies, his Spirit who lives in you."
> —Romans 8:10-11

God intervenes on behalf of Jesus Christ because Jesus gives permission to God to raise Him from the dead by the Holy Ghost.

In order for Jesus to experience loneliness and pain Jesus had to come to this world, but He could not come legally without a body. Jesus had to operate legally in this world. God prepared the birth of a body that was called Jesus and that made it legal through the birth of a body by a woman. Mary the woman produces Jesus' body through her womb. Christ the anointed one is the Spirit.

> "And she shall bring forth a son, and thou shalt call His name Jesus: for He shall save His people from their sins. 22 Now all this was done; that it might be fulfilled which was spoken of the Lord by the prophet, saying, 23 "Behold, a virgin shall be with child and shall bring forth a Son, and they shall call His name Immanuel, which being interpreted is God with Us.
> —Matthew 1:21-23

John tells us 1:13-14 "Which were born, not of blood, nor the will of the flesh, nor the will of man, but God. 14 And the Word was made flesh, and dwelt among us, (and we beheld His glory, the glory as of the only begotten of the Father,) full of grace and truth.

> *"Therefore let all the house of Israel know assuredly, that God hath made that same Jesus, whom ye have crucified, both Lord and Christ."*
> —Act 2:36

So Jesus was the body and Christ was the Spirit. Now Jesus Christ can operate in this physical world legally to regain back the law of dominion back to you, the spirit being having a human experience.

> *"And so it is written, The first man Adam was made a living soul; the last Adam was made a life-giving spirit. Howbeit that was not first which is spiritual, but that which is natural; and afterward that which is spiritual. The first man is of the earth, earthy: the second man is the Lord from heaven And as we have borne the image of the earthy, we shall also bear the image of the heavenly."*
> —1 Corinthians 15:45-49

God knew the outcome of you, a spirit being, dealing with his human experience.

CHAPTER THREE

THE REALM OF EMOTIONS

God understood that your next *spirit being* human experience would be your weakness against Him. Genesis 3:6-13 was that time of weakness and disobedient. This was the beginning of you, the spirit being, to experience weakness and disobedience in your soul, that caused you to go into spiritual warfare. Genesis 3:12 And the man said, "*The woman whom Thou gavest to be with me, she gave me of the tree, and I did eat.*" You, the spiritual being, felt an emotion that you never felt before in your soul and a *portal of guilt* was open. That guilt opens your soul to feel another emotion that you never felt before and that is the emotion of *shame*. Genesis 3:13 states, "*And the Lord said unto the woman, What is this that thou hast done? And the woman said, "The serpent beguiled me, and I did eat.*" She felt an emotion that she never felt before in her soul and a portal of guilt was open. That guilt opened the soul woman's emotion to feel another emotion that she never felt before, and that was shame.

Shame opens the portal of sin. Now both the man

and woman spiritual beings were feeling guilt and shame. And that starts the snowball effect into play. In this snowball effect of guilt and shame another portal opened and that was to blame someone else besides themselves.

> *"And the man said, 'the woman whom Thou gavest to be with me, she gave me of the tree, and I did eat'. And the Lord said unto the woman, 'What is this that thou hast done?' And the woman said, 'the serpent beguiled me, and I did eat.'"*
> *—Genesis 3:12-3:13*

Disobedience affected both the spiritual man and spiritual woman causing a snowball of emotions and blame. This snowball of emotion has been handed down, throughout time, by the first spirit man and his helpmate. The spirit being woman, has been reproducing guilt, shame, and blame after your humankind until today.

As a spirit being, one also experiences the human emotions of belief. The quiet moments in your busy life that allow you to inwardly reconnect with the belief that you are an eternal spirit. If you believe that you are a spirit being first having a human experience, then your soul is considered to enter into a divine peace.

> *"And the Lord God formed man formed man of the dust of the ground, and breathed into his nostrils the breath of life, and man became a living soul."*
> *—Genesis 2:7*

As being part of God's divine will, God breathed into your lifeless beautifully lump of dust and God shaped you into something special. God did not speak a word over your dust body, God did not command your dust body, God did not summon His Holy Ghost nor His angels to bring that beautiful lump of dust to life. God did not even blow on you. If God would have blown on you that beautiful lump of dust, God would scatter you that lump of dust into the air.

Just as carefully as God formed you that beautiful lump of dust, God was careful on how He would bring you to life. When God breathed *in* you that beautiful lump of dust God performed a wonderful miracle. And that miracle was in God's breath that He so carefully breathed into your nostrils. God breathed His personal miracle DNA into you that beautifully lump of dust. DNA is the main component of chromosomes and is the material that transfers genetic characteristics in all life forms. The genetic information of DNA is encoded in the sequence of the bases and is transcribed as the strands unwind and replicate. One of your nostrils was not able to hold all that DNA of God. So, God breathes His DNA into both of your nostrils to balance the DNA into your beautiful body. You were made on the inside of God as part of His spiritual make up. God could not speak over you that lump of dust because there was no DNA in His word.

The angels had no DNA, but God Himself had His DNA. That is why God had to breath into your nostrils carefully with the right amount of breath not to blow up the lump of dust with too much pressure. It was God's DNA that started the miracle chain reaction of you that lump of dust to come alive. Your blood, your blood cells, your lungs, your heart, your brain, your eyes, and your limbs started moving and blood flowing. Your Heart pumping, your brain thoughts started activating. That beautiful lump of dust miracle begins, you to reason, you to walk, you to eat, you to drink as the other animals that God created.

As a spirit being you are having the human experience. You find yourself experiencing all kinds of emotions in your soul. You may wonder where all these emotions are coming from. Your spirit man is here to experience this life and its lessons. How can you fully understand the emotions of unconditional love, forgiveness, compassion, peace, happiness and let harmony reside inside of you?

Your spiritual man expresses your human experience through your soul emotions. Your human experience is in your soul emotions. Lessons you experience in good and wrong motives. Your soul man that experiences these emotions sometimes is led by your natural emotions which are called your flesh. Your human experience in your flesh causes you to misuse your emotional ability.

Your spiritual man that is experiencing human soul emotions are good emotions because God made them. Everything starts with God. Does God have any emotions? If He does, what kind of emotions does God have?

Yes, God has emotions. When you say that God has emotions are you saying that God has emotions as you do. You must understand that what you are seeing in scripture is God relating to you in terms you can understand, and this includes God having emotions. God has revealed His emotions to you in His Bible.

The emotions that God has is perfect and without sin. You are made in the image and likeness of God Genesis

1:26-27 "And God said, Let us make man in Our image, after Our Likeness: and let them have dominion over the fish of the sea, and over the fowl of the air, and over the cattle, and over all the earth, and over every creeping thing that creepeth upon earth. So God created man in His image, in the image of God created He him; male and female created He them." God is full of emotions. It took love emotions to create you in His image and likeness. If God has emotions, then you have emotions. When God breathes life into Adam God gives this spiritual man in this dust body to have free will in his choice that Adam made. Adam was the first to experience human experience that he was misled by his emotions which led to exhibiting disobedience to God.

Because you are reproduced in the likeness and image of Adam the spiritual man in a dust body, Adam DNA was transferred down from generation until today to you the modern-day spiritual man in a dust body. Therefore, you are born a spiritual being in a dust body that you are shaped in disobedient and wickedness. Now you experience human soul emotions. Because of sin, your soul's emotions are touched by sin. You know that God's emotions are not touched by sin.

There is a difference between God's emotions and the spiritual being soul emotions in a dust body. You are made in the image and likeness of God, but your soul emotions were touched by sin and God's emotions were and never will be touched by sin.

There is a lesson to learn for you, the spiritual man. That you can overcome this wickedness in your human experience by operating first as a spiritual being. Your spiritual man is made whole and made without sin because God is without sin. But the human soul experience, that you the spiritual man experience, is a weakness in the emotions of the flesh. Jesus Christ, the Son of God, while in His human form overcame the emotion of wickedness though the temptation of Satan by fasting for forty days and resisting Satan by the word of God.

In Luke 4:14 *"And Jesus returned in the power of the Spirit into Galilee: and there went out a fame of Him through all the region round about."* Jesus Christ was a God Spiritual Being, that was born in a dust body, and walked the world like you and I. Jesus, a God Spiritual Being, in a dust body experienced a range of human experiences while in this world. Jesus Christ, the God, is an example to you as a spiritual being to overcome the weak emotions in your soul to operate in your given dominion in this world.

So Jesus Christ had to experience weakness in the flesh to know what you were going through in the flesh. When Jesus came looking for His friend Lazarus who was asleep. Mary, Lazarus' sister was weeping, the Jews also were weeping. When Jesus saw where they had laid Lazarus His friend John 11:35 says, Jesus wept. Jesus Christ, the God, felt what you feel in your soul emotions. Jesus Christ, the God, had to feel the pain of sadness, disappointment, the loss, and the hurt. So that you, as a spirit being, too can overcome these human soul emotions you experience. God created us to have dominion over the emotional realm as well.

Even as the earthly high priest that Jesus was, He was not touched with weakness as you are. But yet, Jesus Christ the God, was tempted in all points of temptations as you are tempted in your soul weakness, but Jesus was without sin.

Because Jesus was also tempted by wicked desires to cause His weakening emotions to surface up in Him, to give in to Satan temptations. Jesus portrays how to overcome this weakness. Because you are a spirit being that still has a connection with God. Jesus spoke the word of God to defeat wickedness. In you is the word of God, you know God in the spirit because you are a spirit being part of God.

Where do your emotions arise from? Your emotions come from your beliefs and concerns that produced your emotions. Do you know that the soul emotions you are having by your spiritual man are revealing your deepest beliefs and concerns? It is your spirit man that gives your soul man new desires and concerns. *Your spiritual man's godly desires and concerns coupled with your godly beliefs produce godly emotions.*

Scriptures teach you, the spiritual man, that your soul's emotions are central to your life in Christ. That certain emotions, as a spiritual being, you experience are either righteous or sinful. And that you, spiritual man, must manifest righteous emotion and dispense sinful emotions from your soul.

Jesus exhibits some of the very same perplexing emotions we deal with, such as *anger.* Matthew 21:12 *"And Jesus went into the temple of God, and cast out all them that sold and bought in the temple, and overthrew the tables of the moneychangers, and the seats of them that sold doves."* Jesus felt a righteous anger, and this is why He overturned the money-changers' tables who were making His Father's house a "den of robbers." Jesus exhibits *sadness.* John 11:35 "Jesus wept." He felt a deep sorrow over the death of his friend Lazarus. Jesus exhibits *suffering* Luke 22:42-44 "Saying, Father, if Thou be willing, remove this cup from Me: nevertheless not My will, but Thine, be done. And there appeared an angel unto Him from heaven, strengthening Him. And being in an *agony* He prayed more earnestly: and His sweat was as it were great drops of blood falling to the ground." Jesus was suffering from the pain of dying on the cross. These are some of the human soul experiences as a spiritual man you will experience.

You are living in two worlds at the same time. Your human soul experience lives in the natural world and the spiritual lives in the spiritual world. The natural and spiritual world they both co-exist together. Your natural world that you live in consists of everything you can see such as houses, streets, the sky, people etc. Your spiritual world consists of realities that you cannot see such as Jesus, heaven, hell, and angels etc.

If you carefully look at yourself in the mirror and you will realize that your spiritual identity is not something you just imagine. Your natural world is forever reminding you that you are having a human soul experience with your five senses. Your spiritual man in your dust body having human experience with your five senses, that are telling you what you hear, see, feel, smell, touch and taste. In this human experience in the natural world, without realizing it, you can easily become a highly critical human being that is more concerned with body image and other worldly issues than the state of your spiritual man.

Right now, your spiritual man, (in your dust body that is experiencing human soul experiences) might be experiencing unhappiness, depression, and disappointment with yourself. This human experience comes from a lack of knowledge about yourself. You do not see yourself or know yourself to be a spiritual being adopting a human soul experience.

You as a spiritual being experience human soul experiences; you are to appreciate the value of learning and growing at a spiritual level. If you miss this opportunity to discover who you are, you will experience the same type of problems over and over again. Until you learn the lessons that are being presented to you through your human life experience, you will never learn these lessons are always positive and are always for your growth and fulfillment to your higher levels. When you operate from the position that *as a spiritual being having human soul experiences* that are challenging, your human experience in life is a blessing. You see opportunity for growth in everything and not just for yourself but for others as well. So how you overcome human experience weakness is by growing spiritually and not stopping when it gets hard.

There is one human emotional experience that you, as a spiritual being, experience strongly. When you as a spirit, your soul, and your flesh was created and that emotional experience is love. Love is the core nature of you. *You feel good when you give and receive love because this is a spiritual thing to do.* This is you, the spiritual man, your desire is to love. That love is to tend to your spiritual man so that you can regain control of your human soul experiences. Love makes the human soul experience a beautiful thing.

Love is beautiful because God, your Father and creator, made you out of love as a husband and wife. Who laid down and with the glory of sex experience made their child from that love. There was thought and clever design for you, the spirit being to fit into your physical body without blemish and spot on it or in it body.

As a spiritual being having human experiences there is one emotion we struggle to master and that is anger.

Angry emotion is a strong feeling of annoyance, displeasure, or hostility. God gets angry Psalm 106:40. *"Therefore was the wrath of the Lord kindled against His people, insomuch that He abhorred His inheritance."* The anger of the LORD has burned against His people. And God has stretched out His hand against them and struck them down. The reason God gets angry is because of the strong feeling of displeasure that His people provoked Him to anger. This is an emotion that God allows you, as a spiritual being, to experience in your human soul experience so that you will know His strong feelings of displeasure and disapproval. When Satan annoys you, you should feel a strong sense of being annoyed. God said when He committed this human dust body to house your spirit being which is the likeness of Him. How can you be like God without any emotions? As God's anger burned against His people and God struck them down, so should your anger should burn against Satan and all his evil forces. Your anger should not burn against one another but against the things that cause them to walk out of the will of God. *Those things that easily beset you.* Those things that cause you to fall to your temptations. Those things that have a stronghold on you. Those things that keep you ignorant of the truth of the word of God. Those things that cause you to forsake righteousness and walk with the ungodly men. These are the things you, as a spiritual being, experience while you are in your human soul experience. This is the same emotion that God experiences in displeasures with His people.

Is it ok to get angry? The Bible says in Ephesians 4:26 *"Be ye angry, and sin not: let not the sun go down upon your wrath."* It is okay to get angry. It is okay to feel displeasure, it is okay to be annoyed, but you must release that anger. God knows what anger can do to you if you continue to hold on to it. Even God releases His anger. Psalm 106:44-45 *"Nevertheless He regarded their affliction when He heard their cry: And He remembered for them His covenant and repented according to the multitude of His mercies."*

You as a spirit are experiencing the human soul experience in love and emotion. These love emotions, feelings, or actions come from God. God is love, 1John 4:16-19 *"And we have known and believed the love that God hath to us. God is love: and he that dwelleth in love dwelleth in God, and God in him. Herein is our love made perfect, that we may have boldness in the day of judgment: because as He is, so are we in this world. There is no fear in love; but perfect love casteth out fear: because of fear hath torment. He that feareth is not made perfect in love. We love Him because He first loved us."* John 3:16 *"For God so loved the world, that He gave His only begotten Son, that whoever believes in Him should not perish, but have eternal life,"*

But God demonstrates His love toward us, Romans 5:8 *"But God Commendeth His love toward us, in that, while we were yet sinners, Christ died for us."* The Bible tells us to love as in Mark 12:30-31, *"And thou shalt love the Lord thy God with all thy heart, and with all thy soul, and with all thy mind, and with all thy strength: this is the first commandment. And the second is like, namely this, Thou shalt love thy neighbor as thyself. There is none other commandments greater than these."*

Even as a spirit being in your human emotions, you should hate unrighteousness. We should not hate each other but hate the things that God hates. Psalm 5:5 *"The foolish shall not stand in thy sight: Thou hatest all workers of iniquity."* Psalm 11:5 *"The LORD trieth the righteous: but the wicked and him that loveth violence His soul hateth,"*

You, as a spirit being in your human emotions, experiences *compassion*. God is compassionate. Romans 9:15 *"For He saith to Moses, I will have mercy on whom I will have mercy, and I will have compassion on whom I will have compassion."* Exodus 33:19 *"And He said, "I Myself will make all My goodness pass before you, and will proclaim the name of the LORD before you; and I will be gracious to whom I will be gracious, and will show compassion on whom I will show compassion."*

You, as a spirit being, experience the human soul emotion of *grief*. God grieved. Genesis 6:6-7, *"And it repented the Lord that He made man on the earth, and it grieved Him at His heart. And the Lord said, "I will destroy man whom I have created from the face of the earth; both man, and beast, and the creeping thing, and the fowls of the air, for it repenteth Me that I have made them."*

You, as a spirit being, in your human emotions experiences *joy*. God expresses His joy. Zephaniah 3:17, *"The Lord thy God in the midst of thee is mighty; He will save, He will rejoice over thee with joy; He will rest in His love, He will joy over thee with singing."*

So, does God have emotions? Absolutely, yes, He does. God who made you in His image and likeness then has these emotions that you are feeling.

Your emotions differ somewhat from God's because of the sin that touches your emotions. As a spiritual being having these human soul experiences, you experience confusion, uncertainty, delusion, doubt, loss, unworthiness, or apathy, because of the mental battle that is in your head. These manifest out of the wrong thoughts and choices that you make because of the influence and the control of sin over your mind.

CHAPTER FOUR

FREE WILL TO MAKE A CHOICE

If you go back to the Garden of Eden when the serpent spoke to the woman Eve in Genesis 3:2 *"Now the serpent was more subtle than any beast of the field which the Lord God had made. And he said unto the woman, 'Yea, hath God said, Ye shall not eat of every tree of the garden?'"*

All the serpent did was pose a suggestion to Eve (*God said you shall not eat of every tree in the garden?*). Suggesting a question to Eve that you can use your free will and make your own choices. The serpent knew that he could not get Adam to eat from the wrong tree because of his free will. So he figured that if he could get the woman to choose with her free will that he would accomplish two things. First to get her to eat then secondly, she would get Adam to make a choice to eat or not to eat. Get Adam to go against his free will to eat and that would bring chaos between man and God.

The woman replied In Genesis 3:2-3, *"And the woman said unto the serpent. We may eat of the fruit of the tree of the garden: But of the fruit of the tree which is in the midst of the garden, God hath said, Ye shall not eat of it. Neither shall ye touch it, lest ye die.*

Here is where the serpent infiltrated the soul's emotionand realm and a mind war was begun in the human race. In the beginning, man's flesh, his soul, and his spirit were in divine agreement emotionally with God. There was no war between his flesh man, soul man, and spirit man. They were all in harmony with God, in the garden. Flesh man, soul man, and spirit man communed with God in the cool of the evening.

God iterated in Genesis 2:16-17, *"And the Lord God commanded the man, saying, Of every tree of the garden thou mayest freely eat: But of the tree of the knowledge of good and evil, thou shalt not eat of it: for in the day that thou eatest thereof thou shalt surely die."*

God equipped humankind with a free will to choose between right and wrong. Satan wants so badly to destroy what God has made and dearly loves. That was the same freedom that caused the emotion of *pride* to rise up in Satan because God would not allow Satan to have His throne and kingdom.

Since Satan could not have God's throne and kingdom he decides to destroy humankind by luring them into disobedience causing them to worship him instead. But, how was Satan going to do that? The only plan that Satan had was to separate humankind from God. Satan knew that God loved you and was protecting you. So that was not the way. He thought long and hard on how to destroy you and cause you to be separate from God. Satan uses the serpent to do his work. Satan had a plan, and that plan is still working today and he achieves that end by using your soul's emotions against you.

When Satan sent the serpent to tempt the woman his ultimate goal was to separate humankind from God. And Satan did just that! Satan offered the woman a chance to use her free will in Genesis 3:4-5 by saying to her, *"And the serpent said unto the woman, Ye shall not surely die: For God doth know that in the day ye eat thereof, then your eyes shall be opened, and ye shall be as gods, knowing good and evil.*

Satan was correct, the eyes of the human race were opened with emotions and that was the portal opening for the flesh man, soul man, and the spirit man to enter into an emotional conflict. That conflict was the beginning of being separated from God. In God's eye, you were dead to Him, Satan had accomplished his goal on humankind.

> *"And when the woman saw that the tree was good for food and that it was pleasant to the eyes, and a tree to be desired to make one wise, she took of the fruit thereof, and did eat, and gave also unto her husband with her, and he did eat. And the eyes of them both were opened, and they knew that they were naked: and they sewed fig leaves together, and made themselves aprons."*
> —Genesis 3:6-7

This is where the flesh man usurps your free will and now is controlling your soul man. This is the beginning of war within the spirit man and soul man with desires of pleasantness in order for the *flesh* to feel good. That is why, *as a spiritual being*, you are experiencing human soul free will warfare in your mind. In this human soul experience warfare, God still allows your soul man to have free will to make the right choice. Your free will is not dead as Satan is trying to speak to your soul man.

> *"therefore the Lord God sent him forth from the garden of Eden, to till the ground from whence he was taken. So He drove out the man, and He placed at the east of the garden of Eden Cherubims, and a flaming sword which turned every way, to keep the way of the tree of life."* —Genesis 3:23-24

This is the death of humankind. So God sent angels to protect the garden of Eden because God knew that the spirit in you would yearn to return home. This is why the spirit being in you always desires to serve God. This is why the spirit separates himself from the flesh man and the soul man.

> *"For we are strangers before Thee, and sojourners, as were all our fathers: our days on the earth are as a shadow, and there is none abiding."* —1 Chronicles 29:15

This is your spiritual being experiencing the spiritual citizenship experience. That you are just passing through this physical world. Your human soul experience is one with your spiritual free will experience about your heavenly citizenship. Your soul is urging you that this is your home. ***Disobedience serves to deny you of your rightful citizenship so you can instead become a citizen of the satanic kingdom.*** Ephesians 2:19 states, "Now therefore ye are no more strangers and foreigners; but fellow citizens with the saints, and of the household of God."

Your human soul experience does not want you to experience your spiritual citizenship, so that you will not understand or leverage your heavenly citizenship.

Your flesh also wants to serve its own desire and pleasure. Here is the beginning of death, separation from God. In Genesis 3:17 God said, *"And unto to Adam He said, Because thou hast hearkened unto the voice of thy wife, and hast eaten of the tree, of which I command thee, saying thou shalt not eat of it. Cursed is the ground for thy sake; in sorrow shalt thou eat of it all the days of thy life."*

This curse was passed down to you in your human soul experience and not the spiritual man. Because God cannot separate Himself from Himself because the spiritual man is a part of God. This death separation is for you as your human soul begins to experience your loneliness from God. This emotion of *loneliness* in your human soul experience exists to bring back the harmony of the flesh man, soul man, and spirit man. Your spiritual man will long to have an experience with God so that you can build an intimate relationship with God.

Not only was man's soul separated from God, but his family was separated from God for his part in his free will disobedient to God. As a spiritual being having a human soul experience, your action affects your whole family in what you do. You bring a general curse on your family not because of what Satan is doing to you but what you are not doing for God. Curse is on your family. Genesis 3:16 says, "unto the woman He said, I will greatly multiply thy sorrow and thy conception; in sorrow thou shalt bring forth children; and thy desire shall be to thy husband, and he shall rule over thee." Because of her disobedience to God not to her husband. Because she looks upon the tree of good and evil with pleasant eyes in her human soul free will experience. Now God causes her to look at her husband in her humane soul experience with the desire of rule over her. But her spiritual being, and her husband's spiritual being are still equal in the eyes of God.

> *"There is neither Jew nor Greek,*
> *there is neither bond nor free, there is neither male nor female;*
> *for ye are all one in Christ Jesus."*
> —Galatians 3:28

God even cursed this dust body that houses your spiritual being. Genesis 3:19 *"in the sweat of thy face shalt thou eat bread, till thou return unto the ground; for out of it wast thou taken: for dust thou art, and unto dust shalt thou return."* Once God, as King, cursed something it cannot be changed or undone because it is His law. As spiritual beings experiencing the human soul free will experience in your dust body there is sickness and diseases. Sickness and diseases is the body cursed. This causes your body to return to dust for where it came from. Your human house is doomed. But your spiritual being still needs a body to continue to operate in.

CHAPTER FIVE

THE NEW GARDEN OF EDEN

For you, *as a spiritual being,* needed to continue to have a human soul free will experience to show your love toward God. God, in the beginning, created you to house your human soul experience, but you contaminated your house. So, God in all His wisdom and knowledge created another body for you to continue to have your human soul experience. 1 Corinthians 15:53 *"for this corruptible must put on incorruption, and this mortal must put on immortality."* This is where God created you a new body that is not cursed and it did not come from the ground that was cursed by Him. God does not deal with stuff that is flawed and cursed.

There is an eternal house that is not built by hands. 2 Corinthians 5:1-2 *"For we know that if our earthly house of this tabernacle were dissolved, we have a building of God, a house not made with hands, eternal in the heavens. For in this we groan, earnestly desiring to be clothed upon with our house which is from heaven."*

This eternal house will never perish and never be corrupted as was the body that came from the dust and was cursed and corrupted. This will bring your new flesh man and soul man in harmony with your spiritual man, and all will be in harmony with God. You are never separated again from God. In this, you will live forever. It was not time for humankind to live forever from the tree of knowledge of good and evil because of the corruptible flesh body; God knew that it was going to be corrupt. God allows you to make choices by your own free will. Because of the human experiences you are experiencing as a spiritual being, your loneliness from God that your human soul experience feels that it is separation from God, but not your spiritual man. Your spiritual man wants your human soul experience to continue to have the human soul free will experience to show your love toward God. Meaning we can use the power of choice to bring us into a deeper relationship with God.

When God removes humankind from the garden of Eden, God in all His wisdom and knowledge created another Garden Eden. Jesus brought you the new garden of Eden. And that new garden of Eden is the kingdom of God, it is your next Garden of Eden. The kingdom of God is the key element of the teaching of Jesus in the New Testament. This principle is from the Old Testament teachings. God saw that the garden was abandoned by humankind because of corruption. So God creates a new garden, His kingdom, that is solely for those who are *His* children. Everybody will receive an incorruptible body that will not perish, but all will not enter in to the new kingdom. Whether you are a saint or sinner you will receive your incorruptible body. God has promised that everyone that does His will, will enter into the new Garden of Eden.

When you are translated from a corruptible body into an incorruptible one, your new flesh man houses your spiritual man and soul man and this unity brings you into union with God. This is the spiritual experience that you experience in your human soul experience. Your spiritual experiences in your incorruptible body brings you back where you belong in the garden with God. The human soul experience is that you now feel that you belong to God, in His presence, In His worship, and in His praise. 1 Corinthians 15:52-53 *"In a moment, in the twinkling of an eye, at the last trumpet shall sound, and the dead shall be raised incorruptible, and we shall be changed. For this corruptible must put on incorruption, and this mortal must put on immortality."*

But all of you will not see the new Garden of Eden kingdom with your new translated incorruption body because you did not do the will of the Father who is in heaven. Mathew 7:21-23 Jesus said, *"Not every one that saith unto Me, Lord, Lord, shall enter into the kingdom of heaven; but he that doeth the will of My Father which is in heaven. Many will say to Me in that day, Lord, Lord, have we not prophesied in Thy name? and in Thy name have cast out devils? and in Thy name done many wonderful works? And then will I profess unto them, I never knew you: depart from Me, ye that work iniquity."* So, Jesus, your creator will profess your flesh man, soul man, and your spiritual man that He knew you not. Because your flesh man and your soul man are not in harmony with the will of God. You are still separate from the Father, and this is your last chance to get into harmony with the Father. Now the wrath of God is upon you and your punishment is in the lake of fire, that will be your new garden of Eden kingdom.

You don't want your spiritual being experienced having the human soul experience to die the second death. If you are a spiritual being that God made, then you shall be able to control your human soul experience. God gave Adam and Eve dominion as in Genesis 1:26 *"And God said, Let Us make man in Our image, after Our likeness: and let them have dominion over the fish of the sea, and over the fowl of the air, and over the cattle, and over all the earth, and over every creeping thing that creepeth upon the earth."*

Then your spiritual being experience has power over your human soul experience, you shall take control of your human soul experience. If you don't do that then you will be in the category as Revelation says, Rev. 21:8 God said, *"But the fearful, and unbelieving, and the abominable, and murderers, and whoremongers, and sorcerers, and idolaters, and all liars, shall have their part in the lake which burneth with fire and brimstone: which is the second death."* If your human soul experience is not put in check, it will cause your spiritual experience to be out of balance with God's will. And that will cause your name not to be in the book of life. Rev. 20:15 *"And whosoever was not found written in the book of life was cast into the lake of fire."*

CHAPTER SIX

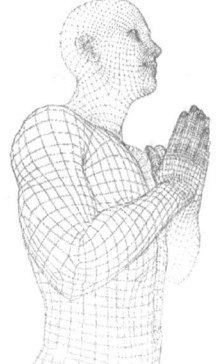

THE INVISIBLE GOD INSIDE OF YOU

1 Corinthians 15:44-48 tells us that the first man was not spiritual but natural, then after came the second man who was spiritual—from heaven. *That which is earthly is earthly and that which is heavenly is heavenly.* In essence there are two images; one earthly and one heavenly.

There is an image that God put into man when He formed his earthly body and that image you have in you, and it comes from God. 1 Corinthians 15:49 points to Genesis 1:26 *"And God said, Let Us make man in Our image, after Our likeness: and let them have dominion over the fish of the sea, and over the fowl of the air, and over the cattle, and over all the earth, and over every creeping thing that creepeth upon the earth."*

You don't know which image you are carrying on the inside of you. I say to you there is something invisible that God put in your house that wants to behold God's image. Because you don't know which image is predominantly operating invisibly in you (on that revelation knowledge), you face problems glorifying God. You face a problem praising your savior Jesus Christ, you face problems being obedient to the Holy Ghost. You don't know the makeup or DNA that is operating in you.

This is where *confusion* comes into play. You don't know of who is the image that is invisible inside of you. I don't want you to carry the image of Satan in you. I don't want you to be like Satan in any kind of way. If you carry Satan's image in you, you are a murderer and a liar—that is his image.

In order for you to know what image that you carry in you, You really need to understand 1Corinthians 15:49 *"And as we have borne the image of the earthly, we shall also bear the image of the heavenly."*

This verse tells you that you carry the image of the earthly which is visible and that is your nature, but you also carry the image of the heavenly that is invisible and that is the image of God. And as we have borne the image of the earthly, but you have the image of Adam and that is a visible body that is subject to infirmities and death. Your body becomes physically weak and has a lack of strength. Your body became incapacitate and that resulted in your sickness in your body. Your nature of disobedience is visible against God that the world sees your real image that is on the inside of you.

You carry the visible image of Adam when you try to hide from God when you have sin. You carry the visible image of Adam when you try to blame someone for your mistake. You carry the visible image of Adam when you don't repent for your sin, but you want to put it on your spouse. That is the visible image on the inside of you.

Verse 49 gives you hope in the midst of the visible

image of Adam on the inside of us. you carry another image on the inside of you.

Verse 49 says, We shall also bear the image of the heavenly. God gave you the power to create in yourself a new heart. To let the visible image of Jesus be seen in you. In your heart you have to release the new visible man after Jesus Christ likeness and the image. God spoke a law about you when He said Let Us make this man just like us with all of Our likeness. God spoke to you so that you can be visible. So God created a physical body with it naturally and put His spirit in this body to be visible. and you are the spitting image of an invisible God made visible. If God is a Spirit, then you are a spirit that God made.

If you want to see God, then look at yourself. Because you are the spitting image of God. I am talking about the invisible God that made Himself visible though you.

1 Corinthians 15:49 says, *"we shall also bear the image of the heavenly."* It is not talking about the heavenly stars or the moon, or the sun or the planets but it points to John 14:9 *"Jesus saith unto him, Have I been so long time with you, and yet hast thou not known Me, Philip? He that hath seen Me hath seen the Father, and how sayest thou then, show us the Father?"*

Jesus was telling Philip that the invisible Father was now visible in Him. Jesus is the spitting image of God the Father. In other words his reply inferred, *If you want to know the Father, then know Me because I am just like Him.*

John 14:9 also points to John 17; the whole chapter is a prayer by Jesus. Let's do what Jesus says about Him knowing the Father and our eternal life (read the whole chapter).

Does someone know you long enough to see the love of God and the image of Jesus in you, to realize that you are the spitting image of the invisible God? Have you been around them long enough for them to see the resemblance of the invisible God in you?

Do you know that you have the visible likeness of Jesus Christ upon your body in the resurrection? When you are fashioned like Jesus and seeking after a greater likeness to Christ that image is visible in righteousness and true holiness.

"So then they that are in the flesh cannot please God. But ye are not in the flesh, but in the Spirit, if so be that the Spirit of God dwell in you. Now if any man have not the Spirit of Christ, he is none of His. And if Christ be in you, the body is dead because of righteousness. But if the Spirit of Him that raised up Jesus from the dead dwell in you, He that raised up Christ from the dead shall also quicken your mortal bodies by the His Spirit that dwelleth in you." —Romans 8:8-11

The Holy Ghost is looking for the image of Jesus Christ in you when the Holy Ghost raises you from the dead so that you can spend time with Jesus.

God created a physical world, so the invisible image of God that is you, yes, your spirit man is invisible. You need a physical body to operate in this physical world so that you can be visible.

God knew you before you were combining with your physical body to be born in this physical world of His. You need to be visible for the world to see that they who don't believe can believe in God.

As God spoke to Jeremiah in Jeremiah 1:5 *"Before I formed thee in the belly I knew thee; and before thou camest forth out of the womb I sanctified thee, and I ordained thee a prophet unto the nations."* Jeremiah was a spirit before he came into his mother's womb. His spirit was combining with his physical body to carry the image of the invisible God to speak the words of the invisible God to the physical nations.

Even Jesus who came to this world, came the same way you did. Jesus came through the womb of a woman. Mary, the woman who bore Jesus Christ, her son, carried His physical body. Matthew 1:18 says, *"Now the birth of Jesus Christ was on this wise: When His mother Mary was espoused to Joseph, before they came together, she was found with child of the Holy Ghost."* Jesus came into this world with the image of the invisible God for you to know whose image you are carrying in you.

Colossians 3:9-10 says, *"Lie not one to another, seeing that ye have put off the old man with deeds; And have put on the new man, which is renewed in knowledge after the image of Him that created him."*

ABOUT THE AUTHOR

www.ingramcontent.com/pod-product-compliance
Lightning Source LLC
Chambersburg PA
CBHW052125110526
44592CB00013B/1753